Everyday Spelling

Home-School Activities

2

**Scott Foresman
Addison Wesley**

Editorial Offices: Glenview, Illinois • Menlo Park, California
Sales Offices: Reading, Massachusetts • Duluth, Georgia • Glenview, Illinois
Carrollton, Texas • Menlo Park, California

1-800-552-2259
http://www.sf.aw.com

ISBN 0-673-61812-9

Copyright © 2000
Scott Foresman-Addison Wesley, a division of
Addison-Wesley Educational Publishers Inc.
All rights reserved.
Printed in the United States of America.

The pages in this book may be duplicated for classroom
use only without further permission from the publisher.

This publication is protected by copyright and permission
should be obtained from the publisher prior to any
prohibited reproduction, storage in a retrieval system, or
transmission in any form or by any means, electronic,
mechanical, photocopying, recording, or otherwise.
For information regarding permission, write to Scott
Foresman-Addison Wesley, 1900 East Lake Avenue,
Glenview, Illinois 60025.

12345678910-PT-08070605040302010099

CONTENTS

Six Letters to Parents precede the Take-Home activities in this resource book. Each letter is printed in English and in Spanish. They are for use at the beginning of each unit.

Lesson Number	Lesson Title	Master	Page Number	Answer Page Number
Lesson 1	Writing Enough Letters	Home-School 1	1	31
Lesson 2	Words with **c, k,** and **ck**	Home-School 2	2	31
Lesson 3	Beginning **br, gr, st, sw**	Home-School 3	3	31
Lesson 4	Ending **mp, nd, nt, sk, st**	Home-School 4	4	31
Lesson 5	Adding **-s** and **-es**	Home-School 5	5	32
Lesson 7	**Short e**	Home-School 7	6	32
Lesson 8	**Short a** and **Short o**	Home-School 8	7	32
Lesson 9	**Short i** and **Short u**	Home-School 9	8	32
Lesson 10	Adding **-ed** and **-ing**	Home-School 10	9	33
Lesson 11	More Words with **-ed** and **-ing**	Home-School 11	10	33
Lesson 13	Using Just Enough Letters	Home-School 13	11	33
Lesson 14	**Long e**	Home-School 14	12	33
Lesson 15	**Long a**	Home-School 15	13	34
Lesson 16	**Long i** and **Long o**	Home-School 16	14	34
Lesson 17	Vowel Sound in **moon**	Home-School 17	15	34

CONTENTS

Lesson Number	Lesson Title	Master	Page Number	Answer Page Number
Lesson 19	Words with Double Consonants	Home-School 19	16	34
Lesson 20	Beginning **ch, sh, th, wh**	Home-School 20	17	35
Lesson 21	Ending **ch, sh, tch, th**	Home-School 21	18	35
Lesson 22	Words with **ce** and **se**	Home-School 22	19	35
Lesson 23	Adding **-es**	Home-School 23	20	35
Lesson 25	Including All the Letters	Home-School 25	21	36
Lesson 26	Vowel Sound in **out**	Home-School 26	22	36
Lesson 27	Vowel Sound with **r**	Home-School 27	23	36
Lesson 28	More Vowels with **r**	Home-School 28	24	36
Lesson 29	Words That Sound Alike	Home-School 29	25	37
Lesson 31	Compound Words	Home-School 31	26	37
Lesson 32	Contractions	Home-School 32	27	37
Lesson 33	Vowel Sound in **ball**	Home-School 33	28	37
Lesson 34	Vowel Sound with **r** and **l**	Home-School 34	29	38
Lesson 35	Getting Letters in Correct Order	Home-School 35	30	38

LETTER 1 UNIT 1　　　　　　　　　LESSONS 1-5

Dear Family,

Welcome to the *ScottForesman Spelling* program. Your child soon will be learning to spell the words from the first five lessons listed below. You can help your child practice spelling at home by using the following activity. The time you spend on this activity will show your child that you consider learning to spell important.

Pick a Card Print each list word on a three-by-five index card or small sheet of paper. Spread out the cards, facedown, in front of your child. Tell him or her to choose a card, without looking at the word printed on it, and hand it to you. Read the word on the card aloud. Then, have your child spell the word aloud and use it in a sentence.

Sincerely,

Week of ____ Lesson 1	Week of ____ Lesson 2	Week of ____ Lesson 3	Week of ____ Lesson 4	Week of ____ Lesson 5
cap	woke	swing	went	lions
bed	can	break	must	boys
camp	kick	stand	friend	nights
bend	took	bring	hand	dishes
pay	back	brother	desk	girls
for	kind	state	different	lunches
play	sick	sweet	and	streets
fort	like	great	bump	wishes
fat	pack	stick	jump	rooms
sing	could	ground	just	foxes
flat	book	brave	ask	peaches
spring	second	grade	land	boxes

CARTA 1 UNIDAD 1 **LECCIONES 1-5**

Querida familia,

Bienvenidos al programa *ScottForesman Spelling*. Su niño o niña va a aprender pronto a deletrear las palabras de las primeras cinco lecciones, que se encuentran en la lista de abajo. Ustedes pueden ayudarle a deletrear en el hogar haciendo la siguiente actividad. El tiempo que empleen en esta actividad demostrará a su niño o niña que ustedes consideran importante el aprender a deletrear.

Elige una tarjeta Escriban con letras de molde cada palabra de la lista en una tarjeta para fichas (3" x 5") o en una hoja pequeña de papel. Extiendan las tarjetas boca abajo frente a su niño o niña. Díganle que elija una tarjeta, sin mirar a la palabra escrita en ella, y que se la entregue a uno de ustedes. Lean la palabra en voz alta. Luego, indíquenle al niño o niña que deletree la palabra en voz alta y que la emplee en una oración.

Atentamente,

Semana de __ Lección 1	Semana de __ Lección 2	Semana de __ Lección 3	Semana de __ Lección 4	Semana de __ Lección 5
cap	woke	swing	went	lions
bed	can	break	must	boys
camp	kick	stand	friend	nights
bend	took	bring	hand	dishes
pay	back	brother	desk	girls
for	kind	state	different	lunches
play	sick	sweet	and	streets
fort	like	great	bump	wishes
fat	pack	stick	jump	rooms
sing	could	ground	just	foxes
flat	book	brave	ask	peaches
spring	second	grade	land	boxes

Everyday Spelling © Scott Foresman • Addison Wesley

LETTER 2 UNIT 2 — LESSONS 7–11

Dear Family,

Listed below are the spelling words your child will be studying in the next few weeks. The following activity provides an enjoyable way for you to help your child learn these words. Your child will benefit greatly from the time you are giving to spelling practice.

Word Riddles Make up riddles about the list words according to the following pattern. The first line of each riddle should tell about the beginning sound or letter of the list word. The second line should include a rhyming word that tells how the list word ends. The third line should tell how many letters are in the list word. The fourth line should ask a question. Here is an example of a riddle written for the list word *dress*.

> It starts like *drum*.
> It ends like *mess*.
> It has five letters.
> What is the list word? (*dress*)

After your child names the list word correctly, have him or her write or spell it.

Sincerely,

Week of ___ Lesson 7	Week of ___ Lesson 8	Week of ___ Lesson 9	Week of ___ Lesson 10	Week of ___ Lesson 11
when	van	into	want	swim
unless	of	rug	watch	run
getting	sat	its	wanted	swimming
men	rock	shut	watching	running
them	have	if	walk	stop
wet	job	mud	look	hug
leg	that	thing	walked	stopping
dress	clock	gum	looking	hugged
tell	bad	fit	call	drop
let	spot	bug	pick	trip
presents	sad	this	calling	dropped
get	doll	hunt	picked	tripped

CARTA 2 UNIDAD 2　　　　　LECCIONES 7-11

Querida familia,

En la lista de abajo aparecen las palabras para deletrear que su niño o niña va a estudiar en las semanas venideras. La actividad siguiente brinda una forma placentera de ayudar a su niño o niña a aprender estas palabras. Su niño o niña se beneficiará mucho con el tiempo que ustedes le dediquen a practicar deletreo.

Adivinanzas de palabras Inventen adivinanzas acerca de las palabras de la lista siguiendo el patrón siguiente. La **primera línea** de cada adivinanza debe ser acerca del sonido o de la letra inicial de la palabra. La **segunda línea** debe incluir una palabra que rime y que diga cómo termina la palabra. La **tercera línea** debe decir cuántas letras hay en la palabra. La **cuarta línea** debe hacer una pregunta. Éste es un ejemplo de una adivinanza escrita para la palabra de la lista **dress**.

Comienza como **drum**.
Termina como **mess.**
Tiene cinco letras.
¿Sabes ya cuál es? **(dress)**

Después de que el niño o niña diga la palabra correctamente, pídanle que la escriba o la deletree.

Atentamente,

Semana de __ Lección 7	Semana de __ Lección 8	Semana de __ Lección 9	Semana de __ Lección 10	Semana de __ Lección 11
when	van	into	want	swim
unless	of	rug	watch	run
getting	sat	its	wanted	swimming
men	rock	shut	watching	running
them	have	if	walk	stop
wet	job	mud	look	hug
leg	that	thing	walked	stopping
dress	clock	gum	looking	hugged
tell	bad	fit	call	drop
let	spot	bug	pick	trip
presents	sad	this	calling	dropped
get	doll	hunt	picked	tripped

Everyday Spelling © Scott Foresman • Addison Wesley

LETTER 3 UNIT 3　　　LESSONS 13–17

Dear Family,

Your child will soon be learning the words in spelling Lessons 13–17. The words are listed below. You can help your child enjoy spelling by practicing these words together. An activity like the one that follows suggests one way to practice the words and have fun, too.

Puzzle Pairs Use a marker to write each list word across the width of an index card. Then cut the card into two pieces so that each part shows approximately half of the letters of the word. Once the words are all written and the cards cut, mix up the pieces. You and your child should each take four. Place any matching pieces together in front of you. Ask your child to identify the word made with each match. Take turns picking the remaining cards and making matches. Trade cards, if necessary, to make the last few matches.

Sincerely,

Week of ____ Lesson 13	Week of ____ Lesson 14	Week of ____ Lesson 15	Week of ____ Lesson 16	Week of ____ Lesson 17
a lot	feet	away	goat	new
also	Easter	paint	right	blew
scared	eat	take	boat	chew
across	clean	baseball	mind	grew
going	read	stay	throw	knew
was	each	mail	high	room
lived	keep	rain	show	food
always	feel	ate	light	soon
stayed	see	wait	float	moon
next	teeth	may	own	zoo
until	team	way	find	flew
upon	between	make	night	too

CARTA 3 UNIDAD 3   LECCIONES 13-17

Querida familia,

Su niño o niña va a aprender pronto a deletrear las palabras de las lecciones de deletreo 13 a 17, que se encuentran en la lista de abajo. Ustedes pueden ayudar a que su niño o niña a disfrute al deletrear practicando con él o ella esas palabras. Una actividad como la siguiente sugiere una manera de practicar las palabras y divertirse al mismo tiempo.

Rompecabeza de pares Con un marcador, escriban cada palabra de la lista en una tarjeta para fichas. Luego corten las tarjetas en dos de manera que cada parte muestre aproximadamente la mitad de las letras de la palabra. Una vez que las palabras hayan sido escritas y las tarjetas hayan sido cortadas, mezclen todas las piezas. Uno de ustedes y el niño o niña deben tomar cuatro cada uno. Pongan en la mesa las tarjetas que formen una palabra. Pidan al niño o niña que identifique la palabra formada por cada par. Tomen turnos para recoger las tarjetas restantes y formar pares. Intercambien tarjetas, si es necesario, para formar los últimos pares.

Atentamente,

Semana de __ Lección 13	Semana de __ Lección 14	Semana de __ Lección 15	Semana de __ Lección 16	Semana de __ Lección 17
a lot	feet	away	goat	new
also	Easter	paint	right	blew
scared	eat	take	boat	chew
across	clean	baseball	mind	grew
going	read	stay	throw	knew
was	each	mail	high	room
lived	keep	rain	show	food
always	feel	ate	light	soon
stayed	see	wait	float	moon
next	teeth	may	own	zoo
until	team	way	find	flew
upon	between	make	night	too

LETTER 4 UNIT 4   LESSONS 19–23

Dear Family,

In the coming weeks our class will be studying the words in spelling Lessons 19–23. The words for these lessons are listed below. You can help your child practice these words at home. Your child will find activities like the following one to be very helpful.

Word Sandwiches Take turns with your child choosing a list word and identifying the "bread" (the first and last letters of the word) for a word sandwich. The other person should then supply the letters that make up the "sandwich filling" for that word (all the letters of the word, except the first and last letters). Then ask your child to spell or write the complete word.

Sincerely,

Week of ___ Lesson 19	Week of ___ Lesson 20	Week of ___ Lesson 21	Week of ___ Lesson 22	Week of ___ Lesson 23
will	there	catch	nice	baby
Halloween	what	push	use	story
follow	then	inch	once	babies
full	shirt	wash	house	stories
tall	the	reach	race	family
stuff	ship	pitch	horse	bunny
egg	white	much	place	families
carry	child	both	those	bunnies
better	chair	which	dance	pony
add	they	with	please	puppy
pretty	where	crash	these	ponies
happy	check	bath	because	puppies

CARTA 4 UNIDAD 4   LECCIONES 19–23

Querida familia,

En las semanas venideras nuestra clase va a estudiar las palabras de las lecciones 19 a 23, que se encuentran en la lista de abajo. Ustedes pueden ayudar a su niño o niña a practicar esas palabras en el hogar. Su niño o niña descubrirá que actividades como la que sigue son muy provechosas.

Sandwiches de palabra Tomen turnos con su niño o niña para elegir una palabra de la lista e identificar el "pan" (la primera y la última letras de la palabra) para un sandwich de palabra. La otra persona deberá proveer las letras para hacer el "relleno del sandwich" (todas las letras de esa palabra, excepto la primera y la última). Luego pidan al niño o niña que deletree o escriba la palabra completa.

Atentamente,

Semana de __ Lección 19	Semana de __ Lección 20	Semana de __ Lección 21	Semana de __ Lección 22	Semana de __ Lección 23
will	there	catch	nice	baby
Halloween	what	push	use	story
follow	then	inch	once	babies
full	shirt	wash	house	stories
tall	the	reach	race	family
stuff	ship	pitch	horse	bunny
egg	white	much	place	families
carry	child	both	those	bunnies
better	chair	which	dance	pony
add	they	with	please	puppy
pretty	where	crash	these	ponies
happy	check	bath	because	puppies

Everyday Spelling © Scott Foresman • Addison Wesley

LETTER 5 UNIT 5 — LESSONS 25-29

Dear Family,

In the coming weeks, your child will be studying the spelling words listed below. You can be of great service to the learning process by practicing the list words with your child. Enjoy the following activity with your child.

Clue Cards Have your child write each list word on an index card. On the other side of each card, your child should draw a picture of the word or write something about the word. For example, for the word *dog*, your child might draw a picture, for the word *all*, your child might write "I like all animals." Mix up the cards. Then hold up one card at a time with the clue side facing your child. Discuss the clue with your child, and then have him or her spell the list word that matches the clue.

Sincerely,

Week of ___ Lesson 25	Week of ___ Lesson 26	Week of ___ Lesson 27	Week of ___ Lesson 28	Week of ___ Lesson 29
give	out	far	girl	to
really	now	started	were	won
some	about	dark	first	two
through	sound	farm	hurt	one
every	mouse	arm	her	I
whole	our	march	bird	here
you	down	hard	turn	eye
would	town	bark	learn	hear
favorite	round	cart	person	no
very	how	party	turtle	by
their	found	part	heard	know
before	clown	barn	burn	buy

CARTA 5 UNIDAD 5 LECCIONES 25-29

Querida familia,

En las semanas venideras su niño o niña va a estudiar las palabras de deletreo de la lista de abajo. Ustedes pueden ayudar mucho al aprendizaje practicando las palabras de la lista con su niño o niña. Disfruten con él o ella de la siguiente actividad.

Pistas en tarjetas Indiquen a su niño o niña que escriba cada palabra de la lista en una tarjeta para fichas. En el reverso de cada tarjeta el niño o niña deberá hacer un dibujo de la palabra o escribir algo acerca de ella. Por ejemplo, para la palabra *dog* el niño o niña puede hacer un dibujo, y para la palabra *all* podría escribir "I like all animals". Mezclen las tarjetas. Luego, sostengan una tarjeta a la vez, mostrando el lado de la pista al niño o niña. Hablen acerca de la pista con el niño o niña y luego pídanle que deletree la palabra de la lista que corresponde a la pista.

Atentamente,

Semana de __ Lección 25	Semana de __ Lección 26	Semana de __ Lección 27	Semana de __ Lección 28	Semana de __ Lección 29
give	out	far	girl	to
really	now	started	were	won
some	about	dark	first	two
through	sound	farm	hurt	one
every	mouse	arm	her	I
whole	our	march	bird	here
you	down	hard	turn	eye
would	town	bark	learn	hear
favorite	round	cart	person	no
very	how	party	turtle	by
their	found	part	heard	know
before	clown	barn	burn	buy

Everyday Spelling © Scott Foresman • Addison Wesley

LETTER 6 UNIT 6 LESSONS 31-35

Dear Family,

Your child will soon be studying the final spelling lessons in the book. The words for these lessons are listed below. As the end of the school year approaches, I'd like to thank you for the assistance you have given to the learning process. You might want to end the year with the following activity.

A, B, C... or Z? Holding several sheets of paper horizontally, write five or six letters of the alphabet in order across the top of each, starting with A and ending with Z. Line up the sheets in alphabetical order in front of your child. Then, say a list word slowly. Have your child first find the letter of the alphabet with which the list word begins and then write the list word below that letter. Continue the activity until all the list words are written on the alphabetical sheets.

Sincerely,

Week of ____ Lesson 31	Week of ____ Lesson 32	Week of ____ Lesson 33	Week of ____ Lesson 34	Week of ____ Lesson 35
something	there's	bought	apple	caught
everything	here's	brought	another	goes
outside	don't	saw	table	who
birthday	isn't	awful	over	aunt
sometimes	that's	crawl	little	children
myself	we're	draw	other	Christmas
everybody	didn't	thought	people	friends
airplane	wasn't	all	flower	beautiful
inside	it's	ball	after	again
sunshine	they're	fall	ever	said
playground	can't	hall	purple	special
bathtub	I'm	small	under	tried

CARTA 6 UNIDAD 6 — LECCIONES 31-35

Querida familia,

Su niño o niña va a estudiar pronto las lecciones de deletreo finales del libro. Las palabras para esas lecciones se encuentran en la lista de abajo. Al aproximarse el fin del año escolar, me gustaría agradecerles por la ayuda que han brindado ustedes al aprendizaje. Si lo desean, podrían terminar el año con esta actividad.

¿A, B, C... o Z? Sosteniendo horizontalmente varias hojas de papel, escriban cinco o seis letras del alfabeto en orden en el borde superior de cada una, comenzando con A y terminando con Z. Ordenen las hojas en orden alfabético frente al niño o niña. Luego, digan lentamente una palabra de la lista. Pídanle al niño o niña que encuentre, primero, la letra del alfabeto con que comienza la palabra de la lista, y luego que escriba la palabra debajo de la letra. Continúen con esta actividad hasta que todas las palabras de la lista estén escritas en las listas alfabéticas.

Atentamente,

Semana de __ Lección 31	Semana de __ Lección 32	Semana de __ Lección 33	Semana de __ Lección 34	Semana de __ Lección 35
something	there's	bought	apple	caught
everything	here's	brought	another	goes
outside	don't	saw	table	who
birthday	isn't	awful	over	aunt
sometimes	that's	crawl	little	children
myself	we're	draw	other	Christmas
everybody	didn't	thought	people	friends
airplane	wasn't	all	flower	beautiful
inside	it's	ball	after	again
sunshine	they're	fall	ever	said
playground	can't	hall	purple	special
bathtub	I'm	small	under	tried

Everyday Spelling © Scott Foresman • Addison Wesley

HOME-SCHOOL ACTIVITIES

■ Word Bits Write the list word that contains each short word below.

1. end
2. pa
3. lay
4. ring
5. for
6. be

Word Check 1
1. cap
2. camp
3. pay
4. play
5. for
6. fort
7. bed
8. bend
9. fat
10. flat
11. sing
12. spring

■ Hidden Words Circle the hidden list words.

7. t r e f o r c
8. r o t f l a t h
9. l g s i n g e
10. e m p c a p e
11. l e c a m p s
12. i r r f a t e

Make a new word by writing the letter that comes after each circle. It spells something good to eat.

7 __ 8 __ 9 __ 10 __ 11 __ 12 __

Dear Parent,

Please check to see that your child has done this page correctly. Circle any misspelled words and help your child study them.

Tear off the **Word Check** before your child returns this page to class. Use it to help your child study.

Name _____

■ 2 HOME-SCHOOL ACTIVITIES 2 ■

Word Check 2

1. pack
2. book
3. can
4. like
5. kick
6. kind
7. sick
8. took
9. second
10. back
11. woke
12. could

■ **Star Game** Fill in the blanks to form list words. Then write the ★ letters to solve the riddle.

1. ___ o u l d
2. ___ a c k ★
3. ___ i k e ★
4. c ___ n ★
5. to ___ k ★

What is something a guitar player uses?

___ ___ ___ ___
a ___ ___ ___ ___

■ **Missing Words** Draw a line to a list word to finish each phrase.

6. ___ up late   pack
7. be ___   woke
8. ___ a bag   kind
9. ___ a goal   feel
10. ___ sick   kick
11. right ___   book
12. a good ___   back

Dear Parent,

Please check to see that your child has done this page correctly. Circle any misspelled words and help your child study them.

Tear off the **Word Check** before your child returns this page to class. Use it to help your child study.

Name _____

■ 3   HOME-SCHOOL ACTIVITIES   3 ■

■ **Word Game** Play with a partner. Cut out the cards. Write a different list word on each card. Pick one card and say the word aloud. Have your partner spell the word. Then let your partner pick a card. Continue until all the words have been spelled.

Word Check 3

1. brother
2. brave
3. break
4. bring
5. great
6. ground
7. grade
8. stand
9. stick
10. state
11. swing
12. sweet

Dear Parent,

Please check to see that your child has done this page correctly. Circle any misspelled words and help your child study them.

Tear off the **Word Check** before your child returns this page to class. Use it to help your child study.

Name _____

■ 4 HOME-SCHOOL ACTIVITIES 4 ■

Word Check 4

1. friend
2. jump
3. desk
4. must
5. went
6. and
7. ask
8. bump
9. different
10. hand
11. just
12. land

■ **Word Bits** Write the list words that contain these short words.

1. an _____   4. us _____

2. rent _____   5. as _____

3. we _____   6. end _____

■ **Word Groups** Write the list word that goes with the two words in each group.

7. chair, bed, _____

8. head, foot, _____

9. cut, scrape, _____

10. air, water, _____

11. hop, run, _____

12. should, ought, _____

How are your answers and this sentence alike?
Did **H**olly **b**orrow **L**arry's **j**umbo **m**agnet?

_____

_____

Dear Parent,

Please check to see that your child has done this page correctly. Circle any misspelled words and help your child study them.

Tear off the **Word Check** before your child returns this page to class. Use it to help your child study.

Name _____

■ 5   HOME-SCHOOL ACTIVITIES   5 ■

■ Letter Change Change the first letter in each word to make a list word.

1. punches
   ___ ___ ___ ___ ___ ___ ___
   ★

2. beaches
   ___ ___ ___ ___ ___ ___ ___
   ★

3. lights
   ___ ___ ___ ___ ___ ___
   ★

4. toys
   ___ ___ ___ ___
   ★

Write the ★ letters to spell the opposite of **hard**.
___ ___ ___ ___

■ Making Connections Circle the list word in each sentence.

5. The city streets look very clean.
6. I helped Mom wash the dishes.
7. We saw two lions in the zoo.
8. There are three foxes playing.
9. Hector wishes he could play, too.
10. The school has many rooms.
11. How many girls are on the team?
12. Please put the shoes in these boxes.

Word Check 5
1. lions
2. nights
3. girls
4. streets
5. rooms
6. boys
7. peaches
8. dishes
9. lunches
10. boxes
11. wishes
12. foxes

Dear Parent,

Please check to see that your child has done this page correctly. Circle any misspelled words and help your child study them.

Tear off the **Word Check** before your child returns this page to class. Use it to help your child study.

Name _____

■ 7   HOME-SCHOOL ACTIVITIES   7 ■

■ **Word Bits** Write the list word that contains each short word below.

1. less _____

2. hem _____

3. hen _____

4. we _____

5. sent _____

6. me _____

How are your answers and this sentence alike?
Usually **T**im **w**ears **W**ill's **p**urple **m**ittens.

_____

■ **Hidden Words** Circle the hidden list words.

7. d o t e l l i t
8. c a l l e g o t
9. g e t o n i t
10. b u g e t t i n g
11. o r e d r e s s
12. f i l l e t o n

Word Check 7
1. tell
2. wet
3. when
4. dress
5. let
6. unless
7. men
8. them
9. get
10. getting
11. leg
12. presents

Dear Parent,
Please check to see that your child has done this page correctly. Circle any misspelled words and help your child study them.

Tear off the **Word Check** before your child returns this page to class. Use it to help your child study.

Everyday Spelling © Scott Foresman • Addison Wesley

Name _____

■ 8 HOME-SCHOOL ACTIVITIES 8 ■

Word Check 8
1. sat
2. rock
3. job
4. bad
5. of
6. van
7. sad
8. spot
9. clock
10. that
11. doll
12. have

■ **Letter Trade** Change the first letter to make a list word. Draw lines to match.

1. if   rock
2. what   sat
3. lock   bad
4. pat   that
5. lad   of
6. pan   van

■ **Hidden Words** Circle the hidden list word. Then write it.

7. r s j o b f

7. _____

8. t h r s a d l

8. _____

9. d o d o l l o

9. _____

10. t v a h a v e w

10. _____

11. o t f s p o t e

11. _____

12. r o c l o c k r

12. _____

Write the letter that comes after each circle. It spells something that smells nice.

___ ___ ___ ___ ___ ___
 7   8   9 10 11 12

Dear Parent,
Please check to see that your child has done this page correctly. Circle any misspelled words and help your child study them.

Tear off the **Word Check** before your child returns this page to class. Use it to help your child study.

HOME-SCHOOL ACTIVITIES

■ **Making Connections** Circle the list word in each sentence.

1. What is that thing?
2. It does not fit there.
3. Put it into the closet.
4. I don't know if I should.
5. Put it back in its box.
6. Is this the one?

■ **Missing Words** Write the list word for each phrase. Rewrite the ★ letters to solve the riddle.

7. a lightning ___ ★___ ___
8. ___ ___ ★___ ___ door
9. vacuum ___ ___ ★
10. scavenger ___ ★___ ___ ___
11. ___ ★___ ___ puddle
12. chewing ___ ★___ ___

What does a bug give its friends?

a ___★___ ___★___ ___★___ ___★___ ___★___ ___★___ ___★___

Word Check 9
1. fit
2. mud
3. this
4. shut
5. rug
6. its
7. gum
8. into
9. thing
10. if
11. bug
12. hunt

Dear Parent,

Please check to see that your child has done this page correctly. Circle any misspelled words and help your child study them.

Tear off the **Word Check** before your child returns this page to class. Use it to help your child study.

Everyday Spelling © Scott Foresman • Addison Wesley

Name _____

■ 10   HOME-SCHOOL ACTIVITIES   10 ■

Word Check 10
1. want
2. pick
3. walk
4. call
5. look
6. watch
7. wanted
8. picked
9. walked
10. calling
11. looking
12. watching

■ **Before And After** Draw lines to the list words that begin and end like the words on the left.

1. wick   look
2. leak   want
3. weight   pick
4. peak   walk
5. paid   looking
6. long   calling
7. coming   picked

■ **Missing Letters** Fill in the blanks to form list words. Then write the ★ letters to solve the riddle.

8. ___ a ___ k ___ ___
    ★

9. ___ ___ ___ ___ h
       ★

10. ___ ___ n ___ ___ ___
           ★

11. c ___ ___ ___
    ★

12. ___ ___ ___ ___ ___ ___ ___ g
               ★

What kind of dog keeps the best time?

a ___ ___ ___ ___ ___ dog
  ★   ★   ★   ★   ★

Dear Parent,

Please check to see that your child has done this page correctly. Circle any misspelled words and help your child study them.

Tear off the **Word Check** before your child returns this page to class. Use it to help your child study.

11 HOME-SCHOOL ACTIVITIES 11

Break The Code! In the code, each number stands for a letter. Look carefully at the code. Use it to write list words.

1. _d_ _r_ _o_ _p_
   4 18 15 16

2. _s_ _t_ _o_ _p_
   19 20 15 16

3. _h_ _u_ _g_
   8 21 7

4. _s_ _w_ _i_ _m_
   19 23 9 13

5. _t_ _r_ _i_ _p_
   20 18 9 16

6. _r_ _u_ _n_
   18 21 14

7. _s_ _w_ _i_ _m_ _m_ _i_ _n_ _g_
   19 23 9 13 13 9 14 7

8. _t_ _r_ _i_ _p_ _p_ _e_ _d_
   20 18 9 16 16 5 4

9. _d_ _r_ _o_ _p_ _p_ _e_ _d_
   4 18 15 16 16 5 4

10. _s_ _t_ _o_ _p_ _p_ _i_ _n_ _g_
    19 20 15 16 16 9 14 7

11. _r_ _u_ _n_ _n_ _i_ _n_ _g_
    18 21 14 14 9 14 7

12. _h_ _u_ _g_ _g_ _e_ _d_
    8 21 7 7 5 4

Code
1 - a
2 - b
3 - c
4 - d
5 - e
6 - f
7 - g
8 - h
9 - i
10 - j
11 - k
12 - l
13 - m
14 - n
15 - o
16 - p
17 - q
18 - r
19 - s
20 - t
21 - u
22 - v
23 - w
24 - x
25 - y
26 - z

Word Check 11
1. drop
2. hug
3. trip
4. swim
5. stop
6. run
7. dropped
8. hugged
9. tripped
10. swimming
11. stopping
12. running

Dear Parent,

Please check to see that your child has done this page correctly. Circle any misspelled words and help your child study them.

Tear off the **Word Check** before your child returns this page to class. Use it to help your child study.

Name _____

■ 13   HOME-SCHOOL ACTIVITIES   13 ■

Word Check 13
1. also
2. scared
3. until
4. across
5. was
6. going
7. lived
8. next
9. upon
10. always
11. stayed
12. a lot

■ **Word Bits** Write the list word that contains each short word below.

1. go

2. so

3. stay

4. as

5. cross

6. up

7. scare

8. ways

■ **Hidden Words** Circle the hidden list words.

9. s c a n e x t n
10. l l a t l o t i
11. s t a u n t i l c
12. g o i l i v e d e

Make a new word by writing the letter that comes after each circle. It tells the word you would use to describe a good person.

___ ___ ___ ___
9   10   11   12

Dear Parent,

Please check to see that your child has done this page correctly. Circle any misspelled words and help your child study them.

Tear off the **Word Check** before your child returns this page to class. Use it to help your child study.

Name _____

■ 14　　HOME-SCHOOL ACTIVITIES　　14 ■

■ **Word Cousins** Match each group of words to a list word.

1. lips, tongue,   read
2. feel, hear,   see
3. listen, write,   teeth
4. hands, legs,   Easter
5. wash, scrub,   clean
6. Thanksgiving, Christmas,   feet

■ **Star Game** Fill in the blanks to form list words. Write the ★ letters to solve the riddle.

7. ___ ___ t
        ★

8. f ___ ___ l
       ★

9. ___ ___ ___ h
        ★

10. t ___ ___ ___
           ★

11. ___ ___ ___ ___ ___ ___ n
           ★

12. ___ ___ ___ p
      ★

What kind of work does every coach like?

___ ___ ___ ___ ___ ___
 7 8 9 10 11   o r ___
                              12

Word Check 14
1. team
2. keep
3. each
4. read
5. feet
6. between
7. eat
8. see
9. teeth
10. clean
11. feel
12. Easter

Dear Parent,

Please check to see that your child has done this page correctly. Circle any misspelled words and help your child study them.

Tear off the **Word Check** before your child returns this page to class. Use it to help your child study.

Name _____

■ 15 HOME-SCHOOL ACTIVITIES 15 ■

Word Check 15

1. way
2. take
3. rain
4. ate
5. paint
6. away
7. make
8. may
9. mail
10. baseball
11. wait
12. stay

■ **Spelling Maze** Find your way from the school to the library. Write a list word that begins with the letter you see on each tree along the path. Use a word only once.

1. _____
2. _____
3. _____
4. _____
5. _____
6. _____
7. _____
8. _____
9. _____
10. _____
11. _____
12. _____

Dear Parent,

Please check to see that your child has done this page correctly. Circle any misspelled words and help your child study them.

Tear off the **Word Check** before your child returns this page to class. Use it to help your child study.

Everyday Spelling © Scott Foresman • Addison Wesley

13

Name _____

16 HOME-SCHOOL ACTIVITIES 16

Missing Words Write the list word to finish each phrase.

1. ___ ___ ___ ___ in the sky

2. ___ ___ ___ ___ ___ in a pool

3. ___ ___ ___ ___ a ball

4. ___ ___ ___ ___ and tell

Hidden Words Circle the hidden list words.

5. s e n m i n d s
6. o u n c o w n o
7. p r f i n d u
8. l i g h g o a t r
9. h i g l i g h t p
10. g o n i g h t u
11. c h r b o a t s
12. b l u r i g h t s

Write the letter that comes after each circle to find out what a cat who eats a lemon turns into.

a ___ ___ ___ ___ ___ ___ ___ ___
　　5　6　7　8　9　10　11　12

Word Check 16
1. night
2. find
3. show
4. boat
5. high
6. goat
7. throw
8. mind
9. right
10. float
11. own
12. light

Dear Parent,

Please check to see that your child has done this page correctly. Circle any misspelled words and help your child study them.

Tear off the **Word Check** before your child returns this page to class. Use it to help your child study.

Everyday Spelling © Scott Foresman • Addison Wesley

14

Name _____

■ 17 HOME-SCHOOL ACTIVITIES 17 ■

Word Check 17

1. moon
2. new
3. zoo
4. soon
5. flew
6. grew
7. too
8. chew
9. room
10. food
11. knew
12. blew

■ **Letter Trade** Change the first letter in each word to write a list word.

1. boo _____   4. boom _____

2. moo _____   5. crew _____

3. dew _____   6. mood _____

■ **Write a Poem** Complete each line of the poem by writing a list word.

The wind b___ ___ ___ .

The bats f___ ___ ___ .

The clouds s___ ___ ___ ___

Covered the big m___ ___ ___ ___ .

But we k___ ___ ___ ___

Treats we'd soon ch___ ___ !

Dear Parent,

Please check to see that your child has done this page correctly. Circle any misspelled words and help your child study them.

Tear off the **Word Check** before your child returns this page to class. Use it to help your child study.

Everyday Spelling © Scott Foresman • Addison Wesley

Name _____

■ 19 HOME-SCHOOL ACTIVITIES 19 ■

Word Check 19
1. will
2. follow
3. tall
4. full
5. Halloween
6. better
7. pretty
8. add
9. stuff
10. egg
11. happy
12. carry

■ **Sentence Game** Cut out the cards. Write a different list word on each card. Turn the cards facedown. Pick one card. Make up a sentence using that list word. Then let your partner take a turn.

Dear Parent,

Please check to see that your child has done this page correctly. Circle any misspelled words and help your child study them.

Tear off the **Word Check** before your child returns this page to class. Use it to help your child study.

16

Everyday Spelling © Scott Foresman • Addison Wesley

Name _____

■ 20 HOME-SCHOOL ACTIVITIES 20 ■

■ **Scrambled Words** Unscramble the letters to find the list word. Draw a line to match.

1. teerh — child
2. hietw — there
3. achri — the
4. lihdc — white
5. het — chair
6. weerh — where

■ **Missing Letters** Fill in the blanks to form list words. Then write the ★ letters to solve the riddle.

7. ___ ___ ___ ___ k
      ★

8. w ___ ___ ___
       ★

9. s ___ ___ ___
         ★

10. s ___ ___ ___
          ★

11. ___ ___ ___ ___ y
         ★

12. t ___ ___ ___
    ★

What is bought by the yard and worn by the foot?

___ ___ ___ ___ ___ ___ ___

Word Check 20

1. chair
2. ship
3. then
4. what
5. the
6. child
7. where
8. shirt
9. they
10. check
11. there
12. white

Dear Parent,

Please check to see that your child has done this page correctly. Circle any misspelled words and help your child study them.

Tear off the **Word Check** before your child returns this page to class. Use it to help your child study.

17

HOME-SCHOOL ACTIVITIES

■ 21   21 ■

Word Check 21

1. catch
2. reach
3. push
4. bath
5. much
6. wash
7. inch
8. both
9. pitch
10. which
11. crash
12. with

■ **Missing Letters** Add the missing letter to make the list word. Then write the word.

1. ___ash   _____
2. ___each   _____
3. bat___   _____
4. ___rash   _____
5. ___itch   _____
6. wit___   _____

How are your answers and this sentence alike? **W**ill **R**ick **h**ave **C**athy's **p**ink **h**at?

_____

■ **Making Connections** Circle the list word in each sentence.

7. Dad loves both of us.
8. Please push me higher on the swing.
9. Tell me which one you would like.
10. Pablo is one inch taller than his sister.
11. I liked the movie as much as you did.
12. Run backwards to catch the ball!

Dear Parent,

Please check to see that your child has done this page correctly. Circle any misspelled words and help your child study them.

Tear off the **Word Check** before your child returns this page to class. Use it to help your child study.

22 HOME-SCHOOL ACTIVITIES 22

■ Letter Change Make a list word by changing the first letter in each word below.

1. rice
2. whose
3. mouse
4. lance
5. lace
6. worse

Word Check 22

1. house
2. these
3. nice
4. use
5. once
6. horse
7. dance
8. those
9. race
10. because
11. place
12. please

■ Hidden Words Circle the hidden list words.

7. o p l e a s e w
8. b e t h e s e a
9. p o r o n c e l
10. t a p l a c e r
11. d r a u s e u
12. u n b e c a u s e s

Make a new word by writing the letter that comes after each circle. It spells a large sea animal.

___ ___ ___ ___ ___ ___
 7   8   9   10   11   12

Dear Parent,

Please check to see that your child has done this page correctly. Circle any misspelled words and help your child study them.

Tear off the **Word Check** before your child returns this page to class. Use it to help your child study.

■ 23　HOME-SCHOOL ACTIVITIES　23 ■

Word Check 23

1. baby
2. babies
3. family
4. families
5. pony
6. ponies
7. story
8. stories
9. bunny
10. bunnies
11. puppy
12. puppies

■ **Flashcards** Look at each picture. Cut out the cards. Turn each card over. On the back, write the list word that tells about the picture. Have a partner check your spelling.

Dear Parent,

Please check to see that your child has done this page correctly. Circle any misspelled words and help your child study them.

Tear off the **Word Check** before your child returns this page to class. Use it to help your child study.

Everyday Spelling © Scott Foresman • Addison Wesley

Name _____

25 HOME-SCHOOL ACTIVITIES 25

■ **Word Parts** Match the word parts to form list words. Write the words.

1. be   y
2. real   fore
3. ver   ly
4. ev   ite
5. favor   ld
6. wou   ery

1. _____
2. _____
3. _____
4. _____
5. _____
6. _____

■ **Hidden Words** Circle the hidden list word.

7. g y o u t
8. o w h o l e r
9. o d g i v e l
10. j s o m e r s
11. o t h e i r t
12. b t h r o u g h e

Make a new word by writing the letters that come before each circle. The new word tells what you have just done.

a ___ ___ ___ ___ ___ ___ ___ !
  7   8   9   9   10 11 12

Word Check 25

1. very
2. really
3. favorite
4. give
5. every
6. some
7. whole
8. you
9. their
10. before
11. would
12. through

Dear Parent,

Please check to see that your child has done this page correctly. Circle any misspelled words and help your child study them.

Tear off the **Word Check** before your child returns this page to class. Use it to help your child study.

Name _____

■ 26 HOME-SCHOOL ACTIVITIES 26 ■

Word Check 26

1. out
2. now
3. mouse
4. down
5. about
6. round
7. our
8. town
9. sound
10. clown
11. found
12. how

■ **Letter Trade** Change the first letter in each word. Write the list word or words that are formed.

1. pound _____ 2. put _____

_____

3. fur _____

_____

4. house _____

■ **Context Clues** Complete each sentence by writing letters to make list words.

H __ __ about going to t __ __ __ ?
   1   2

Would we go n __ __ ?
                     1

We could leave at a __ __ __ __ 2:00 P.M.
                        3   4

May we see the c __ __ __ ?
                  2

Yes, if she is still d __ __ __ at the mall.
                          1

Write the letter you wrote above each number again to tell what the clown does at the end of her act.

__ __ __ ! __ __ __ __ __ __ !
1 2 1   3 4 2 1

Dear Parent,

Please check to see that your child has done this page correctly. Circle any misspelled words and help your child study them.

Tear off the **Word Check** before your child returns this page to class. Use it to help your child study.

Name _____

■ 27   HOME-SCHOOL ACTIVITIES   27 ■

■ **Word Bits** Write the list word that contains each short word below.

1. car _____   3. star _____

2. arch _____   4. arm _____

■ **Letter Game** Fill in the blanks to form list words. Then write the bold letters to solve the riddle.

5. **b** __ __ __   9. __ __ __ **y**

6. __ **a** __   10. __ **a** __

7. __ **r** __   11. __ __ **r** __

8. __ __ __ **n**   12. __ __ __ **d**

Where do farm animals live?

in a __ __ __ __ __ __ __ __

Word Check 27
1. far
2. dark
3. arm
4. part
5. hard
6. started
7. farm
8. cart
9. march
10. bark
11. party
12. barn

Dear Parent,

Please check to see that your child has done this page correctly. Circle any misspelled words and help your child study them.

Tear off the **Word Check** before your child returns this page to class. Use it to help your child study.

23

Name _____

■ 28 HOME-SCHOOL ACTIVITIES 28 ■

Word Check 28

1. learn
2. her
3. girl
4. turn
5. heard
6. turtle
7. bird
8. person
9. burn
10. first
11. hurt
12. were

■ **Hidden Words** Circle the hidden list words. Then write the words.

1. t u r t l b i r d s

2. p e r h e r a

3. w h a l w e r e t

4. p f i r t u r t l e r

■ **Synonyms** Write the list words that mean the same or almost the same as the underlined words.

5. Jill <u>injured</u> her foot.
6. Bill <u>listened to</u> music.
7. That baby is a <u>young woman</u>.
8. We helped <u>set fire to</u> the log.
9. The team finished <u>before all others</u>.
10. He knew every <u>human</u> in the room.
11. I want to <u>get to know</u> Spanish.
12. Leaves <u>change</u> color in the fall.

5. _____
6. _____
7. _____
8. _____
9. _____
10. _____
11. _____
12. _____

Dear Parent,

Please check to see that your child has done this page correctly. Circle any misspelled words and help your child study them.

Tear off the **Word Check** before your child returns this page to class. Use it to help your child study.

Name _____

■ 29   HOME-SCHOOL ACTIVITIES   29 ■

■ **Concentration** Write a list word on each card. Then cut out the cards. Place them facedown. Work with a partner. Take turns picking cards. Make pairs of words that sound the same.

Word Check 29

1. no
2. know
3. hear
4. here
5. to
6. two
7. by
8. buy
9. I
10. eye
11. won
12. one

Dear Parent,

Please check to see that your child has done this page correctly. Circle any misspelled words and help your child study them.

Tear off the **Word Check** before your child returns this page to class. Use it to help your child study.

25

HOME-SCHOOL ACTIVITIES

■ 31   31 ■

Word Check 31
1. birthday
2. sunshine
3. playground
4. myself
5. airplane
6. bathtub
7. something
8. everybody
9. inside
10. sometimes
11. everything
12. outside

Dear Parent,

Please check to see that your child has done this page correctly. Circle any misspelled words and help your child study them.

Tear off the **Word Check** before your child returns this page to class. Use it to help your child study.

■ **Number Game** Draw a line to match the number sentence to the list word.

1=body 2=thing 3=in 4=some
5=out   6=side   7=times 8=every

1. 3+6   everything
2. 4+7   inside
3. 8+2   sometimes
4. 8+1   something
5. 5+6   everybody
6. 4+2   outside

■ **Letter Game** Fill in the blanks to form list words. Then write each letter in bold type to solve the riddle.

7. **p** ___ ___ ___ ___ ___ ___ ___ ___

8. ___ ___ **r** ___ ___ ___ ___ ___

9. ___ ___ ___ **e** ___ ___

10. ___ ___ ___ **s** ___ ___ ___ **e**

11. ___ ___ ___ ___ ___ ___ **n** ___

12. ___ ___ ___ ___ **t** ___ ___

What is fun to give and to get?

a ___ ___ ___ ___ ___ ___ ___ ___

Name _____

■ 32 HOME-SCHOOL ACTIVITIES 32 ■

■ **Snail Trail** Write a different list word in each game box. Then make a game marker. Play with a partner. Flip a coin. For heads, move 1 space. For tails, move 2 spaces. Say the two words that make up each contraction.

Word Check 32
1. it's
2. that's
3. here's
4. there's
5. don't
6. didn't
7. isn't
8. wasn't
9. can't
10. I'm
11. we're
12. they're

START → ... END

Dear Parent,

Please check to see that your child has done this page correctly. Circle any misspelled words and help your child study them.

Tear off the **Word Check** before your child returns this page to class. Use it to help your child study.

Name _____

33   HOME-SCHOOL ACTIVITIES   33

Word Check 33
1. ball
2. bought
3. saw
4. hall
5. awful
6. all
7. thought
8. small
9. crawl
10. brought
11. draw
12. fall

■ **Word Bits** Write the list words that contain these short words.

1. awl _____   4. raw _____
              _____   _____

2. mall _____   5. rough _____
              _____   _____

3. though _____ 6. ought _____

■ **Hidden Words** Circle the hidden list words. Then write the words.

7. b f a w f u l p   10. s m l a l l n
_____   _____
_____   _____

8. a w l s a w i   11. a l f a b a l l i
_____   _____
_____   _____

9. h a w f a l l c   12. f a l h a l l c
_____   _____
_____   _____

Now write the letter that comes after each circle to make a word for eating outdoors.

___ ___ ___ ___ ___ ___
___

Dear Parent,

Please check to see that your child has done this page correctly. Circle any misspelled words and help your child study them.

Tear off the **Word Check** before your child returns this page to class. Use it to help your child study.

28

Name _____

■ 34 HOME-SCHOOL ACTIVITIES 34 ■

■ **Making Connections** Read the sentences. Underline the list words hidden in other words.

1. Hurry, otherwise we'll be late.
2. He threw the ball overhand.
3. I'll talk to you afterwards.
4. These tablemats are clean.
5. We met at the highway underpass.
6. He planted an evergreen tree.

What letter do all but one of these list words end with?

_____

_____

■ **Missing Words** Write a list word to finish each phrase.

7. a _____ plum

8. one after _____

9. an _____ a day

10. a crowd of _____

11. a _____ bit more

12. a beautiful _____

Word Check 34

1. under
2. apple
3. flower
4. table
5. people
6. after
7. ever
8. purple
9. other
10. over
11. little
12. another

Dear Parent,

Please check to see that your child has done this page correctly. Circle any misspelled words and help your child study them.

Tear off the **Word Check** before your child returns this page to class. Use it to help your child study.

HOME-SCHOOL ACTIVITIES

35 — **35**

Word Check 35

1. goes
2. tried
3. friends
4. beautiful
5. said
6. again
7. children
8. aunt
9. special
10. Christmas
11. who
12. caught

■ Opposites
Draw a line to match each word below with a list word that means the opposite.

1. uncle   caught
2. free   special
3. ordinary   aunt
4. adults   friends
5. ugly   children
6. enemies   beautiful

■ Circle Game
Fill in the blanks to form list words. Then write a letter from each circle to solve the riddle.

7. ◯ __ o
8. s ◯ __
9. ◯ __ __ d
10. ◯◯ __ r
11. __ ◯ __ s
12. __ ◯ __ i __

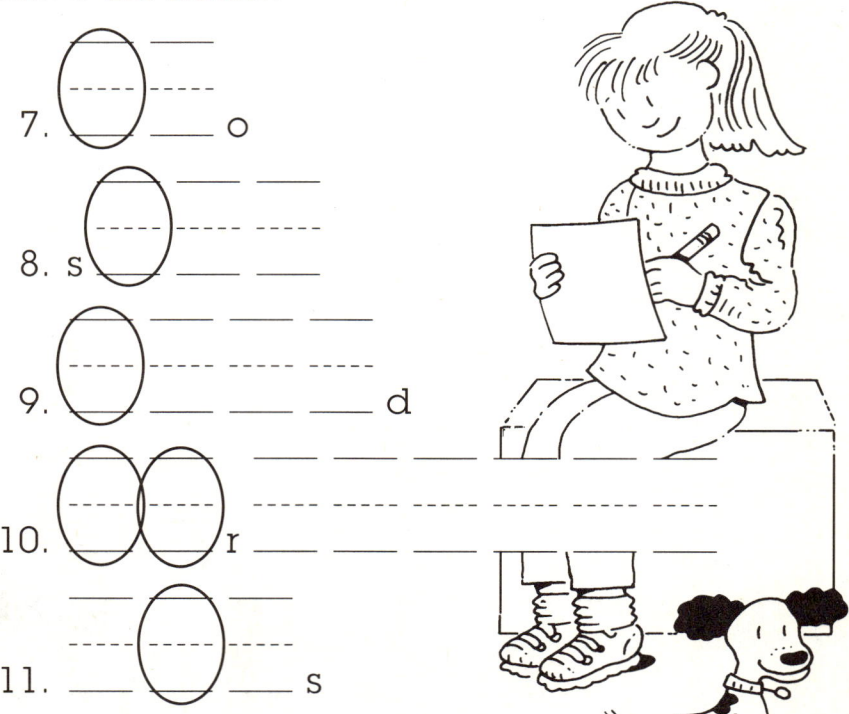

What kind of dog keeps the best time?

a __ __ __ __ __ d __ __
    7 8 9 10 10   11 12

Dear Parent,

Please check to see that your child has done this page correctly. Circle any misspelled words and help your child study them.

Tear off the **Word Check** before your child returns this page to class. Use it to help your child study.

Name _____

■1 HOME-SCHOOL ACTIVITIES 1■

■ **Word Bits** Write the list word that contains each short word below.

1. end — **bend**
2. pa — **pay**
3. lay — **play**
4. ring — **spring**
5. for — **fort**
6. be — **bed**

■ **Hidden Words** Circle the hidden list words.

7. tre f o r c
8. rot l a t h
9. lg s i n g e
10. e m p c a p e
11. l e c a m p s
12. i r r c a t e

Make a new word by writing the letter that comes after each circle. It spells something good to eat.

c	h	e	e	s	e
7	8	9	10	11	12

Word Check 1
1. cap
2. camp
3. pay
4. play
5. for
6. fort
7. bed
8. bend
9. fat
10. flat
11. sing
12. spring

Dear Parent,
Please check to see that your child has done this page correctly. Circle any misspelled words and help your child study them.

Tear off the **Word Check** before your child returns this page to class. Use it to help your child study.

Name _____

■2 HOME-SCHOOL ACTIVITIES 2■

Word Check 2
1. pack
2. book
3. can
4. like
5. kick
6. kind
7. sick
8. took
9. second
10. back
11. woke
12. could

■ **Star Game** Fill in the blanks to form list words. Then write the ★ letters to solve the riddle.

1. _c_ o u l d
2. _P_ a c k
    ★
3. _l_ i k e
    ★
4. c _a_ n
      ★
5. t o _o_ k
        ★

What is something a guitar player uses?

a _p_ _i_ _c_ _k_

■ **Missing Words** Draw a line to a list word to finish each phrase.

6. ___ up late — pack
7. be ___ — woke
8. ___ a bag — kind
9. ___ a goal — feel
10. ___ sick — kick
11. right ___ — book
12. a good ___ — back

Dear Parent,
Please check to see that your child has done this page correctly. Circle any misspelled words and help your child study them.

Tear off the **Word Check** before your child returns this page to class. Use it to help your child study.

Name _____

■3 HOME-SCHOOL ACTIVITIES 3■

■ **Word Game** Play with a partner. Cut out the cards. Write a different list word on each card. Pick one card and say the word aloud. Have your partner spell the word. Then let your partner pick a card. Continue until all the words have been spelled.

3. stick
6. state
9. swing
12. sweet

2. great
5. ground
8. grade
11. stand

1. brother
4. brave
7. break
10. bring

Word Check 3
1. brother
2. brave
3. break
4. bring
5. great
6. ground
7. grade
8. stand
9. stick
10. state
11. swing
12. sweet

Dear Parent,
Please check to see that your child has done this page correctly. Circle any misspelled words and help your child study them.

Tear off the **Word Check** before your child returns this page to class. Use it to help your child study.

Name _____

■4 HOME-SCHOOL ACTIVITIES 4■

Word Check 4
1. friend
2. jump
3. desk
4. must
5. went
6. and
7. ask
8. bump
9. different
10. hand
11. just
12. land

■ **Word Bits** Write the list words that contain these short words.

1. an — **and**   4. us — **just**
2. rent — **different** 5. as — **ask**
3. we — **went**   6. end — **friend**

■ **Word Groups** Write the list word that goes with the two words in each group.

7. chair, bed, — **desk**
8. head, foot, — **hand**
9. cut, scrape, — **bump**
10. air, water, — **land**
11. hop, run, — **jump**
12. should, ought, — **must**

How are your answers and this sentence alike?
Did **H**olly borrow **L**arry's **j**umbo **m**agnet?

Both have words beginning with the same letters.

31

5 — HOME-SCHOOL ACTIVITIES

Letter Change Change the first letter in each word to make a list word.

1. punches
   _l_ _u_ _n_ _c_ _h_ _e_ _s_
                    ★

2. beaches
   _p_ _e_ _a_ _c_ _h_ _e_ _s_
        ★

3. lights
   _n_ _i_ _g_ _h_ _t_ _s_
            ★

4. toys
   _b_ _o_ _y_ _s_
        ★

Write the ★ letters to spell the opposite of **hard**.

_e_ _a_ _s_ _y_

Making Connections Circle the list word in each sentence.

5. The city (streets) look very clean.
6. I helped Mom wash the (dishes).
7. We saw two (lions) in the zoo.
8. There are three (foxes) playing.
9. Hector (wishes) he could play, too.
10. The school has many (rooms).
11. How many (girls) are on the team?
12. Please put the shoes in these (boxes).

Word Check 5
1. lions
2. nights
3. girls
4. streets
5. rooms
6. boys
7. peaches
8. dishes
9. lunches
10. boxes
11. wishes
12. foxes

Dear Parent, Please check to see that your child has done this page correctly. Circle any misspelled words and help your child study them. Tear off the **Word Check** before your child returns this page to class. Use it to help your child study.

---

7 — HOME-SCHOOL ACTIVITIES

Word Bits Write the list word that contains each short word below.

1. less   _unless_
2. hem   _them_
3. hen   _when_
4. we   _wet_
5. sent   _presents_
6. me   _men_

How are your answers and this sentence alike?
Usually **T**im **w**ears **W**ill's **p**urple **m**ittens.

They begin with the same letters.

Hidden Words Circle the hidden list words.

7. d o (t e l l) b i t
8. c a l (l e g) o t
9. (g e t) o n i t
10. b u (g e t t i n g)
11. o r e (d r e s s)
12. f i l (l e t) o n

Word Check 7
1. tell
2. wet
3. when
4. dress
5. let
6. unless
7. men
8. them
9. get
10. getting
11. leg
12. presents

Dear Parent, Please check to see that your child has done this page correctly. Circle any misspelled words and help your child study them. Tear off the **Word Check** before your child returns this page to class. Use it to help your child study.

---

8 — HOME-SCHOOL ACTIVITIES

Word Check 8
1. sat
2. rock
3. job
4. bad
5. of
6. van
7. sad
8. spot
9. clock
10. that
11. doll
12. have

Letter Trade Change the first letter to make a list word. Draw lines to match.

1. if   —   rock
2. what   —   sat
3. lock   —   bad
4. pat   —   that
5. lad   —   of
6. pan   —   van

Hidden Words Circle the hidden list word. Then write it.

7. r s (j o b) f   7. **job**
8. t h r (s a d)   8. **sad**
9. d o (d o l l)   9. **doll**
10. t v a (h a v e) w   10. **have**
11. o t f (s p o t)   11. **spot**
12. r o (c l o c k) r   12. **clock**

Write the letter that comes after each circle. It spells something that smells nice.

_f_ _l_ _o_ _w_ _e_ _r_
 7   8   9 10 11 12

Dear Parent, Please check to see that your child has done this page correctly. Circle any misspelled words and help your child study them. Tear off the **Word Check** before your child returns this page to class. Use it to help your child study.

---

9 — HOME-SCHOOL ACTIVITIES

Making Connections Circle the list word in each sentence.

1. What is that (thing)?
2. It does not (fit) there.
3. Put it (into) the closet.
4. I don't know (if) I should.
5. Put it back in (its) box.
6. Is (this) the one?

Missing Words Write the list word for each phrase. Rewrite the ★ letters to solve the riddle.

7. a lightning   _b_ _u_ _g_
                       ★

8. _s_ _h_ _u_ _t_ door
            ★

9. vacuum   _r_ _u_ _g_
                  ★

10. scavenger _h_ _u_ _n_ _t_
                        ★

11. _m_ _u_ _d_ puddle
         ★

12. chewing _g_ _u_ _m_
                  ★

What does a bug give its friends?

a _b_ _u_ _g_   _h_ _u_ _g_
   ★   ★   ★   ★   ★   ★

Word Check 9
1. fit
2. mud
3. this
4. shut
5. rug
6. its
7. gum
8. into
9. thing
10. if
11. bug
12. hunt

Dear Parent, Please check to see that your child has done this page correctly. Circle any misspelled words and help your child study them. Tear off the **Word Check** before your child returns this page to class. Use it to help your child study.

Everyday Spelling © Scott Foresman • Addison Wesley

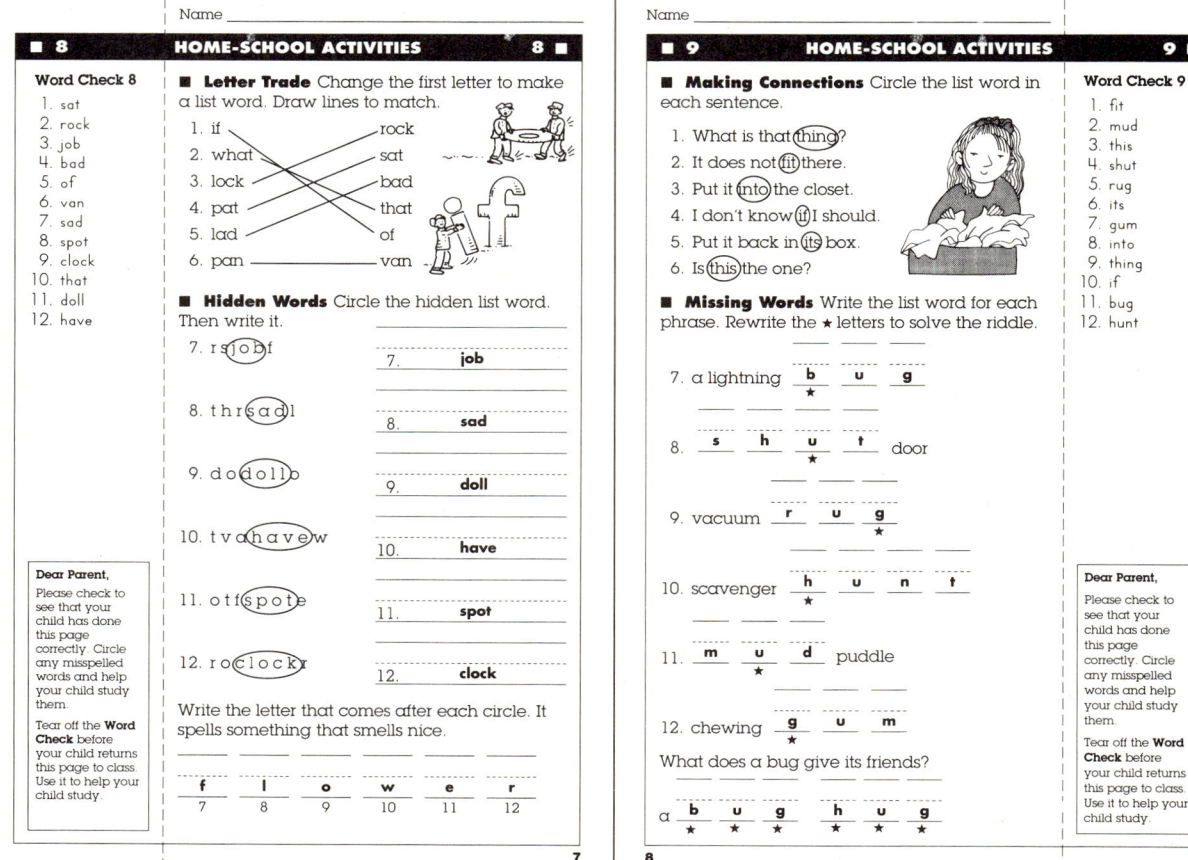

10 HOME-SCHOOL ACTIVITIES 10

Name _____

Word Check 10
1. want
2. pick
3. walk
4. call
5. look
6. watch
7. wanted
8. picked
9. walked
10. calling
11. looking
12. watching

■ **Before And After** Draw lines to the list words that begin and end like the words on the left.

1. wick — look
2. leak — want
3. weight — pick
4. peak — walk
5. paid — looking
6. long — calling
7. coming — picked

■ **Missing Letters** Fill in the blanks to form list words. Then write the ★ letters to solve the riddle.

8. w a l k e d
       ★
9. w a t c h
       ★
10. w a n t e d
           ★
11. c a l l
    ★
12. w a t c h i n g
              ★

What kind of dog keeps the best time?

a w a t c h dog
  ★ ★ ★ ★

Dear Parent,
Please check to see that your child has done this page correctly. Circle any misspelled words and help your child study them.
Tear off the **Word Check** before your child returns this page to class. Use it to help your child study.

---

11 HOME-SCHOOL ACTIVITIES 11

Name _____

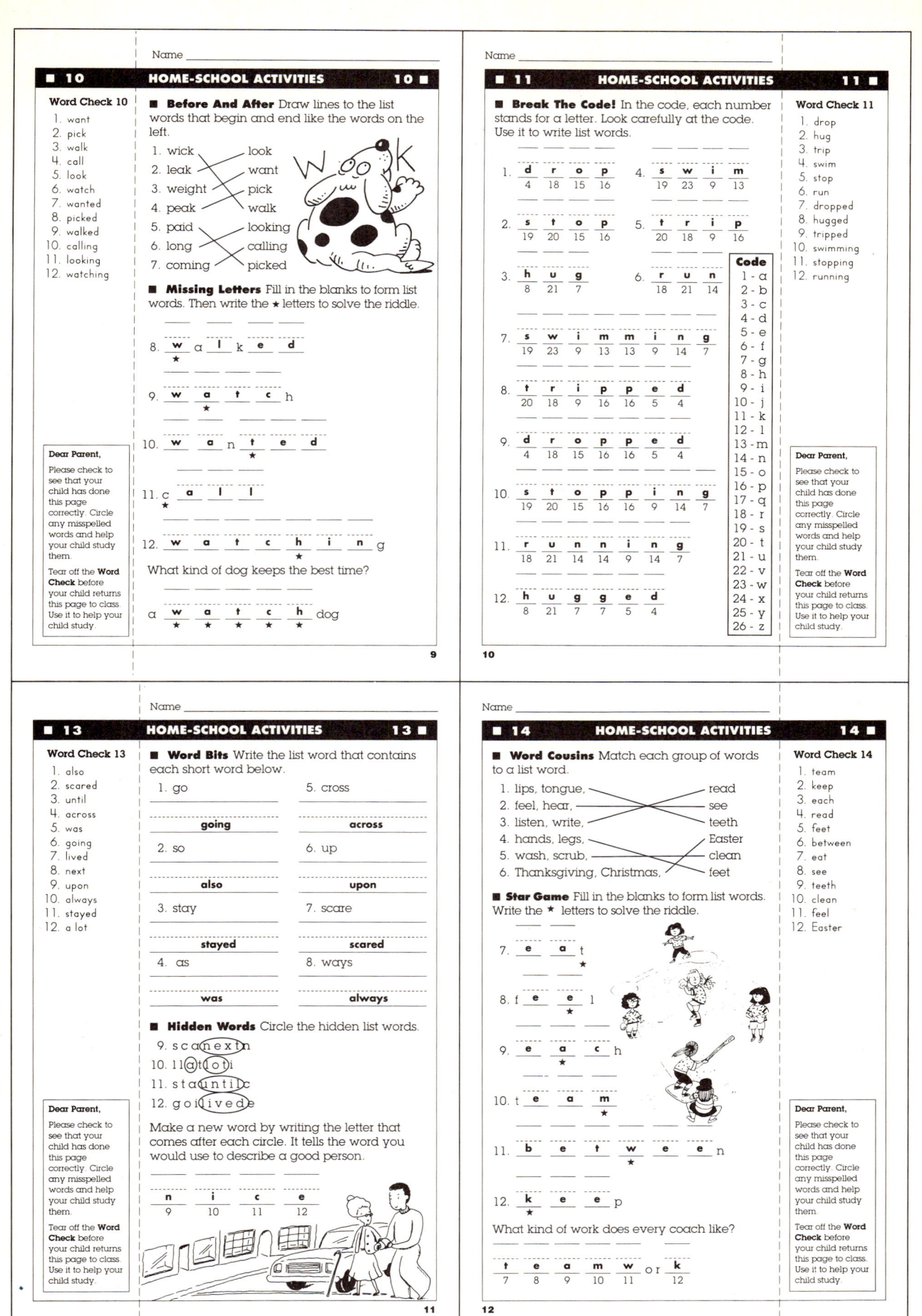

■ **Break The Code!** In the code, each number stands for a letter. Look carefully at the code. Use it to write list words.

1. d r o p   4. s w i m
   4 18 15 16   19 23 9 13

2. s t o p   5. t r i p
   19 20 15 16   20 18 9 16

3. h u g   6. r u n
   8 21 7   18 21 14

7. s w i m m i n g
   19 23 9 13 13 9 14 7

8. t r i p p e d
   20 18 9 16 16 5 4

9. d r o p p e d
   4 18 15 16 16 5 4

10. s t o p p i n g
    19 20 15 16 16 9 14 7

11. r u n n i n g
    18 21 14 14 9 14 7

12. h u g g e d
    8 21 7 7 5 4

Code
1 - a
2 - b
3 - c
4 - d
5 - e
6 - f
7 - g
8 - h
9 - i
10 - j
11 - k
12 - l
13 - m
14 - n
15 - o
16 - p
17 - q
18 - r
19 - s
20 - t
21 - u
22 - v
23 - w
24 - x
25 - y
26 - z

Word Check 11
1. drop
2. hug
3. trip
4. swim
5. stop
6. run
7. dropped
8. hugged
9. tripped
10. swimming
11. stopping
12. running

Dear Parent,
Please check to see that your child has done this page correctly. Circle any misspelled words and help your child study them.
Tear off the **Word Check** before your child returns this page to class. Use it to help your child study.

---

13 HOME-SCHOOL ACTIVITIES 13

Name _____

Word Check 13
1. also
2. scared
3. until
4. across
5. was
6. going
7. lived
8. next
9. upon
10. always
11. stayed
12. a lot

■ **Word Bits** Write the list word that contains each short word below.

1. go   5. cross
   going   across

2. so   6. up
   also   upon

3. stay   7. scare
   stayed   scared

4. as   8. ways
   was   always

■ **Hidden Words** Circle the hidden list words.

9. s c a (next) n
10. l l (a lot) i
11. s t a (until) c
12. g o i (lived) e

Make a new word by writing the letter that comes after each circle. It tells the word you would use to describe a good person.

n i c e
9 10 11 12

Dear Parent,
Please check to see that your child has done this page correctly. Circle any misspelled words and help your child study them.
Tear off the **Word Check** before your child returns this page to class. Use it to help your child study.

---

14 HOME-SCHOOL ACTIVITIES 14

Name _____

■ **Word Cousins** Match each group of words to a list word.

1. lips, tongue, — read
2. feel, hear, — see
3. listen, write, — teeth
4. hands, legs, — Easter
5. wash, scrub, — clean
6. Thanksgiving, Christmas, — feet

■ **Star Game** Fill in the blanks to form list words. Write the ★ letters to solve the riddle.

7. e a t
      ★
8. f e e l
      ★
9. e a c h
      ★
10. t e a m
        ★
11. b e t w e e n
            ★
12. k e e p
      ★

What kind of work does every coach like?

t e a m w o r k
7 8 9 10 11   12

Word Check 14
1. team
2. keep
3. each
4. read
5. feet
6. between
7. eat
8. see
9. teeth
10. clean
11. feel
12. Easter

Dear Parent,
Please check to see that your child has done this page correctly. Circle any misspelled words and help your child study them.
Tear off the **Word Check** before your child returns this page to class. Use it to help your child study.

15 HOME-SCHOOL ACTIVITIES 15

Word Check 15
1. way
2. take
3. rain
4. ate
5. paint
6. away
7. make
8. may
9. mail
10. baseball
11. wait
12. stay

Spelling Maze Find your way from the school to the library. Write a list word that begins with the letter you see on each tree along the path. Use a word only once. **List words beginning with a or m may appear in any order.**

1. stay
2. wait
3. ate
4. baseball
5. take
6. make
7. way
8. paint
9. away
10. may
11. mail
12. rain

Dear Parent,
Please check to see that your child has done this page correctly. Circle any misspelled words and help your child study them.
Tear off the **Word Check** before your child returns this page to class. Use it to help your child study.

16 HOME-SCHOOL ACTIVITIES 16

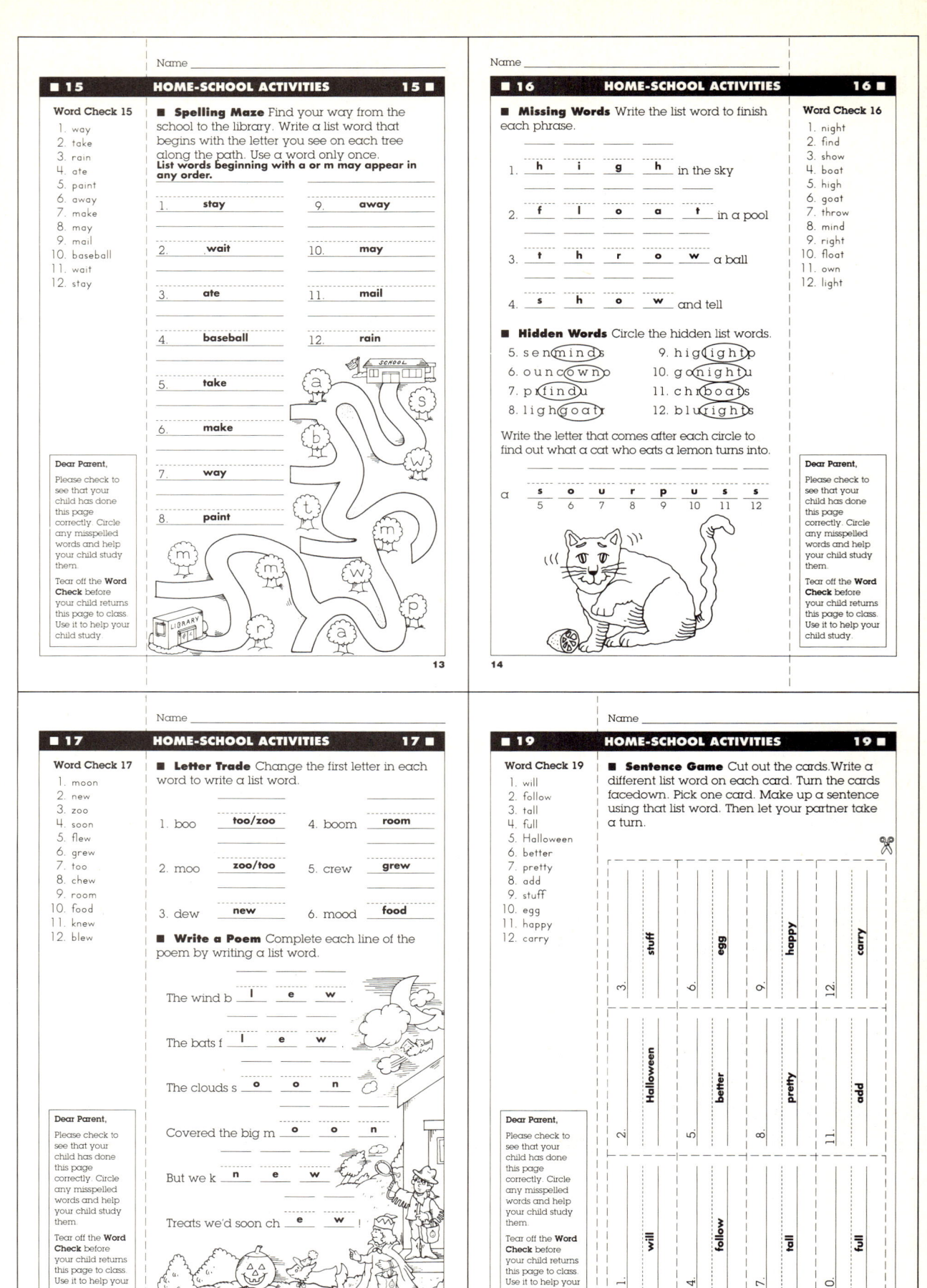

Word Check 16
1. night
2. find
3. show
4. boat
5. high
6. goat
7. throw
8. mind
9. right
10. float
11. own
12. light

Missing Words Write the list word to finish each phrase.

1. h i g h in the sky
2. f l o a t in a pool
3. t h r o w a ball
4. s h o w and tell

Hidden Words Circle the hidden list words.

5. sen(mind)s
6. ounc(own)p
7. pr(find)u
8. ligh(goat)r
9. hig(light)p
10. go(night)u
11. ch(boat)s
12. blu(right)s

Write the letter that comes after each circle to find out what a cat who eats a lemon turns into.

a s o u r p u s s
  5 6 7 8 9 10 11 12

Dear Parent,
Please check to see that your child has done this page correctly. Circle any misspelled words and help your child study them.
Tear off the **Word Check** before your child returns this page to class. Use it to help your child study.

17 HOME-SCHOOL ACTIVITIES 17

Word Check 17
1. moon
2. new
3. zoo
4. soon
5. flew
6. grew
7. too
8. chew
9. room
10. food
11. knew
12. blew

Letter Trade Change the first letter in each word to write a list word.

1. boo — too/zoo
2. moo — zoo/too
3. dew — new
4. boom — room
5. crew — grew
6. mood — food

Write a Poem Complete each line of the poem by writing a list word.

The wind b l e w
The bats f l e w
The clouds s o o n
Covered the big m o o n
But we k n e w
Treats we'd soon ch e w !

Dear Parent,
Please check to see that your child has done this page correctly. Circle any misspelled words and help your child study them.
Tear off the **Word Check** before your child returns this page to class. Use it to help your child study.

19 HOME-SCHOOL ACTIVITIES 19

Word Check 19
1. will
2. follow
3. tall
4. full
5. Halloween
6. better
7. pretty
8. add
9. stuff
10. egg
11. happy
12. carry

Sentence Game Cut out the cards. Write a different list word on each card. Turn the cards facedown. Pick one card. Make up a sentence using that list word. Then let your partner take a turn.

3. stuff	6. egg	9. happy	12. carry
2. Halloween	5. better	8. pretty	11. add
1. will	4. follow	7. tall	10. full

Dear Parent,
Please check to see that your child has done this page correctly. Circle any misspelled words and help your child study them.
Tear off the **Word Check** before your child returns this page to class. Use it to help your child study.

Everyday Spelling © Scott Foresman • Addison Wesley

20 HOME-SCHOOL ACTIVITIES 20

Scrambled Words Unscramble the letters to find the list word. Draw a line to match.

1. teerh — there
2. hietw — white
3. achri — chair
4. lihdc — child
5. het — the
6. weerh — where

Missing Letters Fill in the blanks to form list words. Then write the ★ letters to solve the riddle.

7. c h e c k
8. w h a t
9. s h i r t
10. s h i p
11. t h e y
12. t h e n

What is bought by the yard and worn by the foot?

c a r p e t

Word Check 20
1. chair
2. ship
3. then
4. what
5. the
6. child
7. where
8. shirt
9. they
10. check
11. there
12. white

Dear Parent,
Please check to see that your child has done this page correctly. Circle any misspelled words and help your child study them.

Tear off the **Word Check** before your child returns this page to class. Use it to help your child study.

17

21 HOME-SCHOOL ACTIVITIES 21

Word Check 21
1. catch
2. reach
3. push
4. bath
5. much
6. wash
7. inch
8. both
9. pitch
10. which
11. crash
12. with

Missing Letters Add the missing letter to make the list word. Then write the word.

1. w ash — wash
2. r each — reach
3. bat h — bath
4. c rash — crash
5. P itch — pitch
6. wit h — with

How are your answers and this sentence alike?
Will Rick have Cathy's pink hat?

The missing letters are the same as the first letter of each word in the sentence.

Making Connections Circle the list word in each sentence.

7. Dad loves (both) of us.
8. Please (push) me higher on the swing.
9. Tell me (which) one you would like.
10. Pablo is one (inch) taller than his sister.
11. I liked the movie as (much) as you did.
12. Run backwards to (catch) the ball!

Dear Parent,
Please check to see that your child has done this page correctly. Circle any misspelled words and help your child study them.

Tear off the **Word Check** before your child returns this page to class. Use it to help your child study.

18

22 HOME-SCHOOL ACTIVITIES 22

Letter Change Make a list word by changing the first letter in each word below.

1. rice — nice
2. whose — those
3. mouse — house
4. lance — dance
5. lace — race
6. worse — horse

Hidden Words Circle the hidden list words.

7. o p(please)w
8. be(these)a
9. po r(once)l
10. ta(place)r
11. d r a(use)u
12. un(because)s

Make a new word by writing the letter that comes after each circle. It spells a large sea animal.

w a l r u s
7 8 9 10 11 12

Word Check 22
1. house
2. these
3. nice
4. use
5. once
6. horse
7. dance
8. those
9. race
10. because
11. place
12. please

Dear Parent,
Please check to see that your child has done this page correctly. Circle any misspelled words and help your child study them.

Tear off the **Word Check** before your child returns this page to class. Use it to help your child study.

19

23 HOME-SCHOOL ACTIVITIES 23

Word Check 23
1. baby
2. babies
3. family
4. families
5. pony
6. ponies
7. story
8. stories
9. bunny
10. bunnies
11. puppy
12. puppies

Flashcards Look at each picture. Cut out the cards. Turn each card over. On the back, write the list word that tells about the picture. Have a partner check your spelling.

Dear Parent,
Please check to see that your child has done this page correctly. Circle any misspelled words and help your child study them.

Tear off the **Word Check** before your child returns this page to class. Use it to help your child study.

20

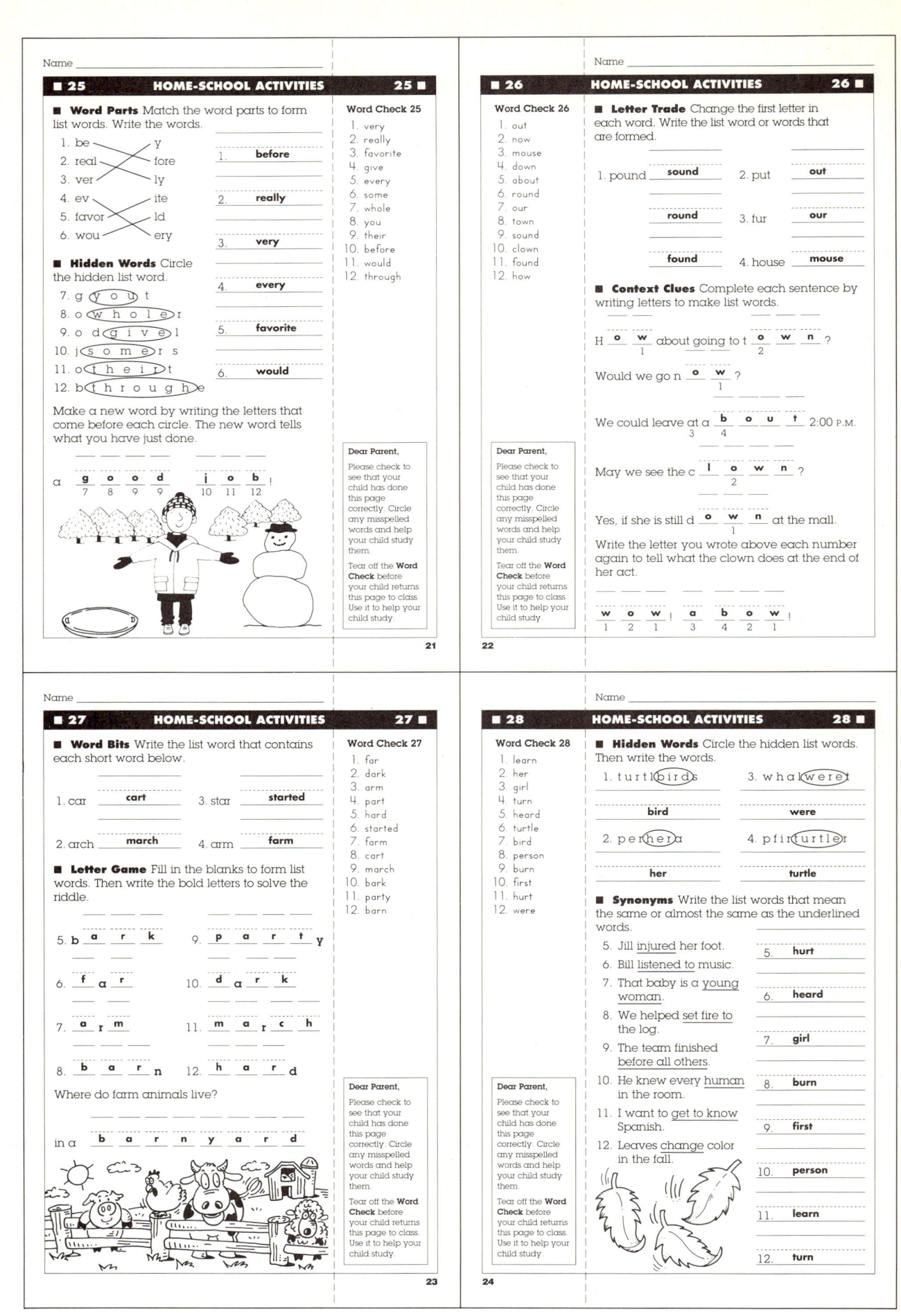

25 — HOME-SCHOOL ACTIVITIES

Word Parts Match the word parts to form list words. Write the words.

1. be — y
2. real — fore
3. ver — ly
4. ev — ite
5. favor — ld
6. wou — ery

1. before
2. really
3. very
4. every
5. favorite
6. would

Hidden Words Circle the hidden list word.

7. g(you)t
8. o(whole)r
9. od(give)l
10. j(some)rs
11. o(their)t
12. b(through)e

Make a new word by writing the letters that come before each circle. The new word tells what you have just done.

a g o o d j o b !
  7 8 9 9 10 11 12

Word Check 25
1. very
2. really
3. favorite
4. give
5. every
6. some
7. whole
8. you
9. their
10. before
11. would
12. through

Dear Parent,
Please check to see that your child has done this page correctly. Circle any misspelled words and help your child study them.
Tear off the **Word Check** before your child returns this page to class. Use it to help your child study.

21

26 — HOME-SCHOOL ACTIVITIES

Letter Trade Change the first letter in each word. Write the list word or words that are formed.

1. pound — sound
2. put — out
   round
3. fur — our
   found
4. house — mouse

Context Clues Complete each sentence by writing letters to make list words.

H o w about going to t o w n ?
  1   2

Would we go n o w ?
             1

We could leave at a b o u t 2:00 P.M.
                     3 4

May we see the c l o w n ?
                      2

Yes, if she is still d o w n at the mall.
                        1

Write the letter you wrote above each number again to tell what the clown does at the end of her act.

w o w ! a b o w !
1 2 1   3 4 2 1

Word Check 26
1. out
2. now
3. mouse
4. down
5. about
6. round
7. our
8. town
9. sound
10. clown
11. found
12. how

Dear Parent,
Please check to see that your child has done this page correctly. Circle any misspelled words and help your child study them.
Tear off the **Word Check** before your child returns this page to class. Use it to help your child study.

22

27 — HOME-SCHOOL ACTIVITIES

Word Bits Write the list word that contains each short word below.

1. car — cart   3. star — started
2. arch — march   4. arm — farm

Letter Game Fill in the blanks to form list words. Then write the bold letters to solve the riddle.

5. b **a** r k   9. p **a** r t y
6. **f** a r   10. d **a** r k
7. **a** r m   11. m **a** r c h
8. **b** a r n   12. h **a** r d

Where do farm animals live?

in a b a r n y a r d

Word Check 27
1. far
2. dark
3. arm
4. part
5. hard
6. started
7. farm
8. cart
9. march
10. bark
11. party
12. barn

Dear Parent,
Please check to see that your child has done this page correctly. Circle any misspelled words and help your child study them.
Tear off the **Word Check** before your child returns this page to class. Use it to help your child study.

23

28 — HOME-SCHOOL ACTIVITIES

Hidden Words Circle the hidden list words. Then write the words.

1. turtl(bird)s — bird
2. per(her)a — her
3. wha(were)t — were
4. pfir(turtle) — turtle

Synonyms Write the list words that mean the same or almost the same as the underlined words.

5. Jill injured her foot. — hurt
6. Bill listened to music. — heard
7. That baby is a young woman. — girl
8. We helped set fire to the log. — burn
9. The team finished before all others. — first
10. He knew every human in the room. — person
11. I want to get to know Spanish. — learn
12. Leaves change color in the fall. — turn

Word Check 28
1. learn
2. her
3. girl
4. turn
5. heard
6. turtle
7. bird
8. person
9. burn
10. first
11. hurt
12. were

Dear Parent,
Please check to see that your child has done this page correctly. Circle any misspelled words and help your child study them.
Tear off the **Word Check** before your child returns this page to class. Use it to help your child study.

24

29 HOME-SCHOOL ACTIVITIES 29

Concentration Write a list word on each card. Then cut out the cards. Place them facedown. Work with a partner. Take turns picking cards. Make pairs of words that sound the same.

I	two	hear
to	know	one
no	won	buy
eye	by	here

Word Check 29
1. no
2. know
3. hear
4. here
5. to
6. two
7. by
8. buy
9. I
10. eye
11. won
12. one

Dear Parent,
Please check to see that your child has done this page correctly. Circle any misspelled words and help your child study them.
Tear off the **Word Check** before your child returns this page to class. Use it to help your child study.

---

31 HOME-SCHOOL ACTIVITIES 31

Word Check 31
1. birthday
2. sunshine
3. playground
4. myself
5. airplane
6. bathtub
7. something
8. everybody
9. inside
10. sometimes
11. everything
12. outside

Number Game Draw a line to match the number sentence to the list word.
1=body 2=thing 3=in 4=some
5=out 6=side 7=times 8=every

1. 3+6 — everything
2. 4+7 — inside
3. 8+2 — sometimes
4. 8+1 — something
5. 5+6 — everybody
6. 4+2 — outside

Letter Game Fill in the blanks to form list words. Then write each letter in bold type to solve the riddle.

7. p **l** a y g r o u n d
8. b **i** r t h d a y
9. m y s **e** l f
10. **s** u n s h i n e
11. a i r p l **a** n e
12. b a **t** h t u b

What is fun to give and to get?

a **p r e s e n t**

Dear Parent,
Please check to see that your child has done this page correctly. Circle any misspelled words and help your child study them.
Tear off the **Word Check** before your child returns this page to class. Use it to help your child study.

---

32 HOME-SCHOOL ACTIVITIES 32

Snail Trail Write a different list word in each game box. Then make a game marker. Play with a partner. Flip a coin. For heads, move 1 space. For tails, move 2 spaces. Say the two words that make up each contraction.

Order of words may vary.

START	END
isn't	it's
can't	I'm
wasn't	that's
didn't	here's
we're	they're
don't	there's

Word Check 32
1. it's
2. that's
3. here's
4. there's
5. don't
6. didn't
7. isn't
8. wasn't
9. can't
10. I'm
11. we're
12. they're

Dear Parent,
Please check to see that your child has done this page correctly. Circle any misspelled words and help your child study them.
Tear off the **Word Check** before your child returns this page to class. Use it to help your child study.

---

33 HOME-SCHOOL ACTIVITIES 33

Word Check 33
1. ball
2. bought
3. saw
4. hall
5. awful
6. all
7. thought
8. small
9. crawl
10. brought
11. draw
12. fall

Word Bits Write the list words that contain these short words.

1. awl — crawl
2. mall — small
3. though — thought
4. raw — draw
5. rough — brought
6. ought — bought

Hidden Words Circle the hidden list words. Then write the words.

7. b f (a w f u l) p — awful
8. a w l (s a w) i — saw
9. h a w (f a l l) — fall
10. s m l (a l l) n — all
11. a l f a (b a l l) — ball
12. f a (h a l l) — hall

Now write the letter that comes after each circle to make a word for eating outdoors.

p i c n i c

Dear Parent,
Please check to see that your child has done this page correctly. Circle any misspelled words and help your child study them.
Tear off the **Word Check** before your child returns this page to class. Use it to help your child study.

Everyday Spelling © Scott Foresman • Addison Wesley

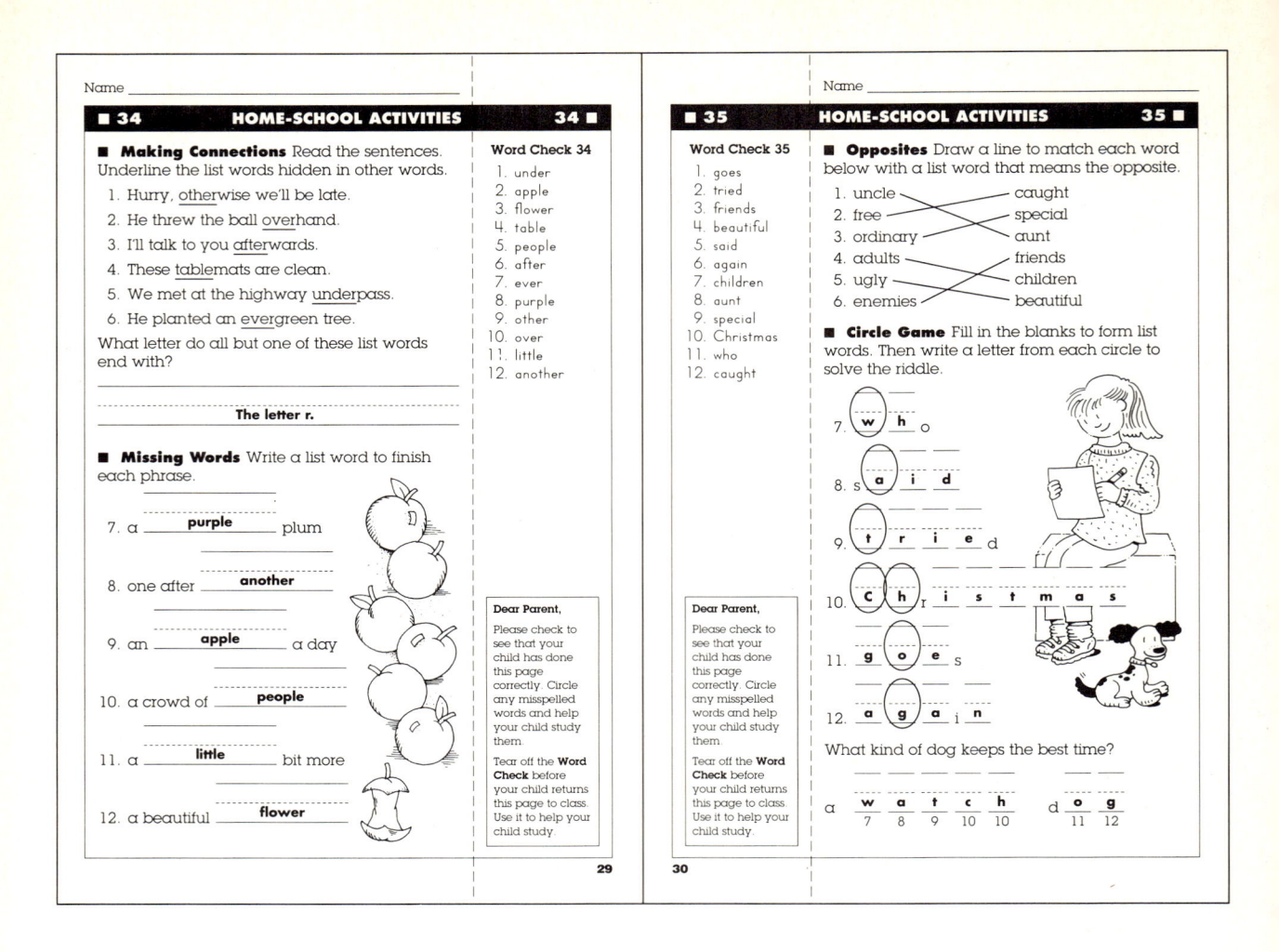

Name _____

■ 34 HOME-SCHOOL ACTIVITIES 34 ■

■ **Making Connections** Read the sentences. Underline the list words hidden in other words.
1. Hurry, <u>otherwise</u> we'll be late.
2. He threw the ball <u>overhand</u>.
3. I'll talk to you <u>afterwards</u>.
4. These <u>tablemats</u> are clean.
5. We met at the highway <u>underpass</u>.
6. He planted an <u>evergreen</u> tree.

What letter do all but one of these list words end with?

_____
__The letter r._____

■ **Missing Words** Write a list word to finish each phrase.

7. a __purple__ plum
8. one after __another__
9. an __apple__ a day
10. a crowd of __people__
11. a __little__ bit more
12. a beautiful __flower__

Word Check 34
1. under
2. apple
3. flower
4. table
5. people
6. after
7. ever
8. purple
9. other
10. over
11. little
12. another

Dear Parent,
Please check to see that your child has done this page correctly. Circle any misspelled words and help your child study them.

Tear off the **Word Check** before your child returns this page to class. Use it to help your child study.

29

Name _____

■ 35 HOME-SCHOOL ACTIVITIES 35 ■

Word Check 35
1. goes
2. tried
3. friends
4. beautiful
5. said
6. again
7. children
8. aunt
9. special
10. Christmas
11. who
12. caught

■ **Opposites** Draw a line to match each word below with a list word that means the opposite.
1. uncle — caught
2. free — special
3. ordinary — aunt
4. adults — friends
5. ugly — children
6. enemies — beautiful

■ **Circle Game** Fill in the blanks to form list words. Then write a letter from each circle to solve the riddle.

7. (w)(h)o
8. s(a)i d
9. (t)r i e(d)
10. (C)h r i s t m a s
11. (g)o(e)s
12. (a)g(a)i n

What kind of dog keeps the best time?

a __w__ __a__ __t__ __c__ __h__ __d__ __o__ __g__
  7 8 9 10 10   11 12

Dear Parent,
Please check to see that your child has done this page correctly. Circle any misspelled words and help your child study them.

Tear off the **Word Check** before your child returns this page to class. Use it to help your child study.

30

38

Everyday Spelling © Scott Foresman • Addison Wesley